TOP DOG

*I dedicate this book to my Butcher
and to the Woman at the end of my Lead*

TOP DOG

A Cavalier View of the English

BY

C. M. McMUCK

OF BUCKLESHAM HALL

AS TOLD TO

FERNAND AUBERJONOIS

WITH ILLUSTRATIONS BY THE AUTHOR

PREFACE BY THE DUKE OF ST. ALBANS

INTRODUCTION BY SUSANNAH YORK

DEBRETT'S PEERAGE LTD.

Semper Fidelis
But Lead Us Not Into Temptation

Text and illustrations © Fernand Auberjonois 1980

Published by Debrett's Peerage Limited
73/77 Britannia Road, London SW6

ISBN 0 905649 39 7

Printed in Great Britain by
The Garden City Press Limited,
Letchworth, Hertfordshire SG6 1JS

Contents

Preface

BY CHARLES FREDERIC AUBREY DE VERE BEAUCLERK, 13TH
DUKE OF ST. ALBANS

Claims of kinship with Charles I and II are many. They call for close scrutiny. A dog's claim does not necessarily lack validity, but that of a dog named McMuck needs to be looked at twice before passing judgment.

This is not to say that a Cavalier King Charles Spaniel is incapable of writing a book. I am not acquainted with the author of this one, but I have known the ghost-writer for many years and I trust his integrity as a note-taker.

The trouble with the breed (King Charles's, not ghost-writers) is a tendency to take over man's domain. Mr McMuck is no exception. I suspect that in his case the takeover of man by dog is without recourse. Man is being dictated to.

Why is it that this Cavalier decides he can only be walked in one of the twelve London parks maintained by the Crown? Why Kensington Palace Gardens? Battersea Park, a precinct of the Greater London Council, a plebeian playground if there ever was one, was good enough for Rupert.

Rupert, named after the Prince of the Rhine (1619–1682) was a Cavalier King Charles who inherited from his namesake a taste for the arts, for languages, for intellectual pursuits . . . and for the ladies. In our coarse modern English he would be called "randy".

Every morning he dragged me across the Albert Bridge in search of attractions. When last observed in action he was courting a black Labrador bitch in Sussex, a county whose name spells half his problems.

Unlike McMuck, Rupert did not consume mountains of chicken. He ate *horse*. When horsemeat began to climb in step with OPEC oil he stopped eating horse. I gather that he lived happily ever after.

[7]

Introduction

BY SUSANNAH YORK

Archy, a present from Michael during my first acting days, was a Cavalier King Charles of genuinely dogged disposition who co-starred with me in *Tom Jones*, *Sebastian*, *Images*, and *The Importance of Being Earnest*. He never became a ham however and – gourmand rather than gourmet – when last seen breaking rules was dragging the Christmas Turkey down our street, at a time when making a living was hard for actresses and turkeys.

Archy kept growing. Having started his meteoric rise as a tiny bundle of white and chestnut fur which could be concealed in an overnight bag on journeys to the Hebrides, he became a substantial dog who made cycling dangerous since he would shift his weight from side to side in the back pannier . . . He eventually learned to jog for his dinner.

And so, jogging behind me on the bicycle, he would take me for walks in Hyde Park. But he *lived* in World's End, a glorious area then, full of barrows and wonderfully chaseable alleycats and with as wonderfully friendly a butcher; an area, in short, too easily dismissed as the "wrong end" of King's Road. For was it not the World's End where Nell Gwynn lived. Where Charles II came to visit? What better address for Archy de Vere, as that descendant of courtiers and Court gossips, Cefn Mawr McMuck, would surely agree.

Unlike McMuck, he could not write. But he was the most *person* dog I ever knew. Greedy (at a sitting he devoured a 6lb box of chocolates, leaving only the violet creams), absent-minded (he was master of the double-take), wonderfully loving and equally wonderfully unsloppy, full of sound and fury though not noticeably brave, Archy was absolutely his own dog, managing his life and usually ours with sturdy sensibility. He played a superb game of hide-and-seek and brushed seriously with the law only once when he was arrested for peeing on a policeman's boot.

From puppystar he evolved into grand old man. But he never entirely broke with his bohemian beginnings: alley-cats remained chaseable till the end and he made as many homes of theatre dressing-rooms as he did of food-trucks on filmsets.

. . . And, by way of anecdote (for his life was full of serendipity), he has become a legend to my children who never knew him. When he died I put on his grave the moss teddy bear sent by one of the Beatles to welcome my first-born, Sasha.

For I still think he died to make way for the new pretender. And I still think some of his spirit went into the making of my divinely dogged daughter. Also, as I daily, enormously recognise the noble tradition, my son Orlando follows in being so very much his own dog . . .

Why Another Book About the English?

"I am His Highness' dog at Kew;
Pray tell me, Sir, whose dog are you?"
(POPE'S EPIGRAM ON A DOG COLLAR)

Better than any other people, the English understand dogs. Therefore no one understands the English better than their dogs.

The special relationship between dogs and Englishmen goes back a long way. Some English dogs are more aristocratic than others – the same as with people. If I sound a bit pompous, narrow, too concerned with the elite, with class, the reason is that I am a *TOP DOG*.

You don't become a Top Dog through effort or special skill. You are born that way. Call us snobs if you wish. The fact is that environment has conditioned our thinking.

In the case of the King Charles Cavalier Spaniel – my breed – the association with the ruling class started as far back as the reigns of Elizabeth I and James. We sat in the laps of Kings and Queens although we had no letters patent. Loyalty doesn't mean servility. We were allowed in rooms from which greyhounds were excluded. Our archives bulge with historical documents.

For a T-D there is something irresistible about a family tree. About ROOTS. We know where we come from.

When I decided to record my impressions of the English, more precisely of Londoners, I was aware of my limitations. No one doubts that dogs can write if they set their mind to it. They have the patience, the stamina, the experience . . . the time. But they need ghost-writers or, more accurately, stenographers.

In my case the limitations are human ones. I depend upon the whims and vagaries of the man I use as typist and literary agent, the man in our house. Without him this essay would not have been published.

He (as I shall refer to him henceforth) is an unreliable assistant, often too busy with his own affairs to pay due attention to mine. But *He* is all I have. *She* has more time for me, but most of it is spent walking or worrying about my health.

The three of us live in a reasonably elegant district of London, The Royal Borough of South Kensington. Our street holds no secrets for me. I have scanned it from one end to the other over a period of eight years. I can tell with my eyes closed what it smells like: Kentucky fried chicken (*née* Fish and Chips), pungent perfumes from Arabia, forsythia, light ale and Scotch egg, Capstan Navy Cut, wet newspapers, horse manure and the dead leaves of autumn.

I use that street as address book, memory bank, computer . . . *Who's Who*. It is where I get my inspiration, my knowledge of the past as it relates to the present.

My study of British mores concerns the relationship between dogs and people today. More people own dogs than ever before. Most Englishmen believe this to be a healthy demographic trend, the sign of a steady evolution towards egalitarianism, like the house, the car, the TV.

I have my doubts about equality. Between man and dog, yes! Among dogs? That is another matter. Top Dogs have background. They are well prepared for the task of analysing the special condition known as *Englishness*. But for this they must be allowed access to the public and not only to the public footpaths. Our voice must be heard.

What is sound to one man is noise to another. Britons enjoy the sound of a dog's voice. They have quiet babies and loud dogs. Our bark is not noise but conversation.

Allow me, then, to get a word in edgewise, first about the past.

King Charles II was the most distinguished of our protectors. Cavaliers were named after him. How thrilling to think that the next Sovereign is to be named after us!

Let me quote from the records: "Being with some kind of his court during his troubles, a discourse arose what sort of dogs deserved pre-eminence. It being on all hands agreed to belong either to the spaniel or the greyhound, the King gave his opinion on the part of the greyhound, because, said he, it has all the good nature of the other without fawning."

The King said this in jest. It was a piece of satire upon his courtiers. Modern Cavaliers do not "fawn". I refuse to believe that our forefathers fawned or fainted. Yet the history books insist they did:

"A lady of my acquaintance had a King Charles Spaniel which, on her return from a lengthened absence devoured her with caresses and then suddenly fell motionless on the hearth-rug. She picked him up.– his eyes turned back in his head and he died instantly."

Such a scene would be unthinkable nowadays. It does prove, however, that in order to make Britain what it is today, a dog's Paradise, our ancestors had to suffer. The Everest of indifference was conquered step by step. Many a brave dog died for the Cause.

Despite occasional royal sponsorship we have had our ups and downs. I understand that in the days of Edward III dogs were not allowed to wander alone in London streets, day or night, *gentlemanly dogs excepted*, under the threat of the owner being fined [40 pence].

What makes dogs gentlemen? My sources define the gentlemanly dog as "Well-bred, not mongrel or cur dog, or perhaps fighting dog used against bear or bull".*

Our name once was the *Spaniell Gentle or Comforter*. A

---

* Bear or bull is meant here literally, not in the sense of the modern expression in use in the money temples.

royal physician listed us as "the Chamber Companion, a pleasant playfellow, a pretty worme . . .". Courtiers were jealous and did their best to distort our image. One William Harrison called us "Instruments of follie to plaie and dallie withall in trifling away the treasure of time, to withdraw their mistresses' minds from more commendable exercizes".

Instruments of follie to plaie and dallie withal.

How pretentious can you get! And I can give you three guesses what "more commendable exercizes" this Harrison chap had in mind. Of course he was committing his hack prose to paper four hundred years ago, but even then he had to admit that we the gentle Cavaliers were "little and prettie and fine, and sought out far and near to satisfy the nice delicacy of dainty dames and wanton women's willes".

We were, and still are, privileged creatures. To survive at the Palace you had to be privileged. Under Henry VIII the Royal Household regulations specified that *Noe Doggs be Kept in Court*. This applied to "greyhounds, mastiffs, hounds . . . but not to small spanyells for ladies or others". I don't know what they mean by *others*.

Charles II decreed that only persons having property amounting to £100 per annum or being sons of a person of higher degree could keep dogs. We, the Cavaliers, qualified . . . and survived.

We survived the Great Plague when the Lord Mayor and Magistrates decreed the destruction of 40,000 dogs and 200,000 cats. We survived such madmen as the Duke of Norfolk who fed spaniel pups to his eagles. We survived the Great Fire. We Overcame!

We have survived sarcasm, edicts, medical obscurantism. To think that we gave our lives to relieve the gout attacks of our masters is hardly credible today. But I have it on good authority that Thomas Lancaster, Archbishop of Armagh, wrote the following prescription for a friend in 1571:

"Take 4 spaniell whelpes four days old, scald them and cause the entrails to be taken out but wash them not. Mix with turpentine, pharmacete, a handful of nettles and a quantity of oil of balme. Put back inside the pups, sew up, roast, take the liquid out and anoint you where your grief is."

Some anointing!

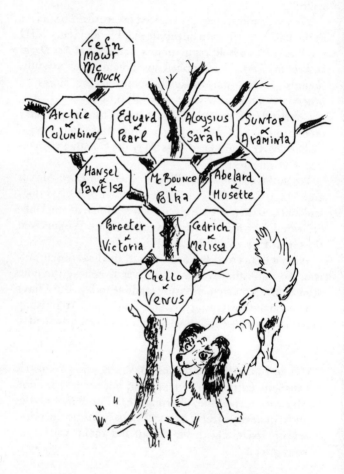

There is something irresistible about a family tree

From Country Dog to City Dog

"They even display traits of character from which mankind themselves might draw examples worthy of imitation".

(PETER PARLEY – *Animals of the Dog Kind; 1837*)

I was born eight years ago in the English countryside near Ipswich, the son of Archie McMuck of Eyeworth and of Cefn Mawr Columbine, thoroughbred King Charles Spaniels. On my father's side I am related to the Pargeters, on my mother's side to the Sunninghills and Pant Isas. Need I say more?

The characteristics of the King Charles Cavalier have been ably and duly catalogued in the literature. We are "a loving breed, extremely intelligent, an intrinsic part of the family". We prefer the company of humans to that of dogs. We are clean and never foul our bed.

I was seven weeks old when my foster-parents came from London to fetch me in East Anglia where I lived at Bucklesham Hall with my brother Archie and my sister Leonora. We shared a basket. In another basket under the kitchen table my mother and several aunts spent most of their time gossiping.

Life at Bucklesham Hall was an Upstairs-Downstairs situation. The older dogs were allowed upstairs for tea, but not us, the puppies. Not class prejudice in this case. Something to do with natural functions.

I remember the English country house as a damp place and the English garden in January as even damper. I have a vague recollection of wet grass, crocuses, foxy smells, rubber boots.

The Englishman upstairs was Army. We didn't see much of him. The Lady was firm but just. Early on she brought in an expert to have a look at me and my siblings.

[17]

This kennel woman had a voice like a foghorn. She wore tweeds reeking of pipe tobacco. Holding me in her powerful hands, flat on my back, she peered at me through thick glasses and pronounced me "A character . . . not dog show quality . . . too many freckles in the wrong places . . . too big . . . wide in the front, turned-in toes, weak pasterns, dipped back . . . gay tail".

Gay tail indeed!

The trouble with English expertise is that it seldom makes allowances for departure from tradition. The English don't like change. They go by the book. Anyway, I wasn't Cruft's material. My mother was humiliated, I was relieved.

On the day of my adoption the two Londoners drove down in a modest Austin but, otherwise, made a good impression. Knowing nothing about dogs they chose me rather than my brother Archie because of my faults and my winning ways. Papers were signed, a cheque changed hands, no cash, a dignified transaction on the whole.

An endless journey to London. I dozed most of the time.

I did observe my new Best Friends when they were not looking. Typical English pushovers for canine charm. I would have no trouble with her. Things might be a bit more difficult with him.

Later on I learned more about English dog lovers. Country dog lovers rough it. Cavaliers are fond of silk, deep chairs, satin coverlets, smoked salmon, walks in well-manicured parks, cocktail parties, new faces. Country dog lovers are inward-looking, practical. They stoke fires while discussing rising damp.

City dog lovers come under two headings: house owners and flat dwellers. Mine, fortunately, resided in a flat – I say fortunately because in a house with garden there is a tendency to push the dog out at regular intervals and leave him to his own devices. The flat has the advantage of the horizontal layout. Man and dog live on a footing of equality. Cavaliers resent relegation to basements.

I settled in quickly. At first *He* thought he could fence me in behind plastic-coated chicken wire in one of the smaller rooms with a floor protected by newspapers. I had other ideas. Little by little I gained access to every corner of this spacious Victorian abode.

From a brief period of paper training I derived considerable benefits in that I became an avid reader of the *Financial Times*, to my mind the best that British journal-

Country dog lovers

ism offers. Even as a puppy I was partial to that pink hue. I never liked the so-called "populars" of tabloid size. But it is all a matter of taste.

From my diary of these early days I find the following lines worth quoting:

— "First night in London spent in a beer crate lined with blanket and pillow. Hot water bottle in corner of improvised bed. In shape of cat, presumably to take the place of brother and sister. Hot cat didn't fool me but, exhausted, I did lean against it and went to sleep. Next morning I overheard them saying they had not slept a wink as they kept waiting for loud cries and yelping that never came."

— "Second night: Howled and howled."

— "Mates easily upset by dog tantrums and weeping fits. Can't tell drama from comedy. They follow the book about Cavaliers which recommends 'extravagant praise' when puppy performs in the right place at the right time. Choruses of 'Good boy!' slightly nauseating."

— "Saw myself in mirror. Not bad for a three-month-old. Strong forepaws, silky coat of white and light brown. Spots over eyes and under nose, moustache-like. Forehead and cheeks generously speckled with beauty spots, Tail not yet a full brush, but long and expressive, twirls like drum majorette's baton in moments of joy."

Humility was not my strong point then. Top Dogs are vain, but they learn to hide their vanity. Again from my diary:

— "Hunger strike to protest against the 'come-and-get-it' attitude of the people in the flat who served meals in a dish marked DOG and didn't pay attention to their guest. Feigned or authentic, hunger strikes included in repertoire of the newly acquired whelp. Man of the house sufficiently worried to get down on his knees and spoon-feed me egg yolk, baby vegetables and raw

One of life's great challenges ... the pigeon behind the frosted glass window

mince. I took my time. Ate from finger-tips. Cavaliers appreciate refinements."

– "Exploration of kitchen during the first, uneventful days. Among the chewable items: garlic cloves, caning on chairs, champagne corks, plastic buttons from a pouf, corner of a wicker basket."

– "Breakfast of cooked cereals. Left alone in the kitchen, therefore ate it. No choice. Rather enjoyed the stuff but didn't show it. Saved face."

– "Growing up. Legs getting longer. Spend much time on the balcony sniffing spring plants and insulting pigeons and blackbirds on chimney pots."

From puppydom to the first traumatic walk on London's pavements. In the words of the Astronaut on the moon, "a giant step".

Late one afternoon *He* came home with a package. Nothing edible, my nose told me. *She* took it away from him as if it contained the crown jewels. I heard the rustle of paper, a sound I love because it is Christmas, a picnic, the butcher shop. *She* squealed with delight: "A MacDonald tartan!"

It was a dog collar. Before I knew it it was around my neck and I was being walked out-of-doors. I summoned all the forces of inertia but she tugged at the lead. I dug in. Then *He* took over and persuaded me of the futility of counter-revolutions.

And so, day after day, night after night, week after week, I began my rounds, from pillar to post, from black garbage bag to black garbage bag, from tyre to tyre, from tree to tree, from gate to gate . . .

But I was not always being led. I learned to call the tune. The English are pushovers. The hard streak in their nature melts away at the sound of a whimper, at the sight of a *beaten dog* expression. I decided I would be the Top Dog in our area, which meant that I had to be first out in the morning, preferably at dawn, rain or shine. Now this is an established practice, a ritual.

Every morning except when I hear a downpour, *She* and I are the only ones enjoying ourselves out there. Correction, there is the Indian family returning from Meditation. Also the drunken gambler weaving an unsteady course to the wrong house, and the newsboy dropping bundles of papers on doorsteps.

Six o'clock. London awakes. A glorious moment!

He, pretending not to hear, is a shapeless mass under the bedclothes.

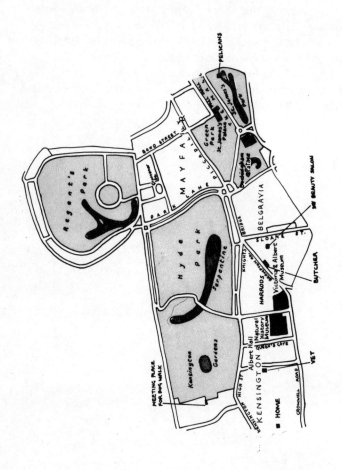

Map of Greater London

Our Royal Parks

> "The faculty by which animals can communicate
> their ideas to each other is very striking; in Dogs it is
> particularly remarkable."
>
> PETER PARLEY – *Tales of Animals*

People who adopt Cavalier King Charles Spaniels need at least two hours exercise daily, in all seasons. London's royal parks were conceived and are maintained for that very purpose.

It is not true that Englishmen don't go on walks unless they have dogs. Dogs simply stimulate walkers and, in this way, contribute to raising the level of the country's general health.

Any London map shows at a glance how small an area the city covers, and how vast are the green expanses. I can walk from Kensington Gardens over to Hyde Park and along that horse ghetto known as Rotten Row, then to Green Park and to St. James's Park and back again, hardly ever putting paw to concrete.

True, Regent's Park has drifted northward, beyond the buffer zone of dwellings and pizza parlours they call Mayfair. If you look at my own personal London plan you will notice that I have brought all parks together, the way they should have been in the first place.

On my first walks in Kensington Gardens, when my legs were too weak for frantic romps, all dogs were giants, except myself. I was both scared and flattered by all the attention. I shivered as they sniffed. The grass was tall. I was too small for a dash after pigeons.

The dogs of England are interpreters, ice-breakers and communicators between humans. Were it not for us, Englishmen would talk mostly to themselves. In the royal parks Londoners speak to other Londoners when securely

Too small to dash after pigeons

tied to Afghans, Schnauzers, Terriers and especially to Cavaliers.

The park is a modern Agora. All news of any consequence spreads through dogs, not cats. Without us there would be total silence, broken only by timid how-do-you-dos, or by the roar of jumbo jets on their approach to Heathrow Airport.

At the age of six months, when I had got over my drunken sailor's gait, I joined a group of London ladies on their morning outings. They were not accompanied by men. Male dog-walkers appeared only at weekends. Those who officiated on weekdays were mostly retired judges, former colonial officials, or gentlemen hen-pecked beyond salvation.

The Kensington Park ladies, or dog-ladies as they are known to park attendants and policemen, congregate be-

[26]

tween 8 and 9 every morning. They identify so completely with their animals that one refers to them as "Luke's mother" or "Titus's guardian".

Most of the talk during these expeditions is about dogs. Class barriers collapse when dog owners come within barking distance of one another, provided the animal is of good breed. The opening gambit seldom varies:

"Boy or girl?"

"Boy, but not aggressive. Yours?"

"Girl, but safe now."

"Who did the altering?"

"Mr. B. of course. I wouldn't go to any other Vet."

"Quite so. And gorgeous-looking."

"Thank you."

"I meant the Vet."

This may lead to further exchanges, or it may not. Without the dog there would have been no dialogue.

Veteran dog-ladies take on the characteristics of their charges. They walk at their dog's pace. Their dog-call is not unlike our bark. Given time they turn into hybrids and take on the characteristics of their charges.

Cavaliers crave admiration. Parks provide unlimited opportunities for social exchanges with appreciative strangers, some of whom, it is true, are too direct and familiar in their approach. An American school teacher in an apricot pant suit will blurt out, "What kinda dog izzat?" The Cockney wife addresses one as Charlie. The effusive Italian tries to date La Signora for lunch. We never accept.

Dog walk conversations can be about matters of secondary importance: food, prices, holidays, politics, how to roast pheasant, whose boy is on drugs.

One of the main features of the park is the round pond, a body of water filled with greenish, tangy water that smells of rotten cabbage. As one dives into it one can feel its warm embrace. An oily substance works itself into the

Given time the dog-ladies take on some of the characteristics of
their charges . . .

pores, matting the hair. More soup than water, really.

Although the round pond has been conceived for our
use and enjoyment, we can only go there when no one is
watching. The place is occupied by swans, bullies of the
first order, who may try to drown us by holding our heads
under the water until our last breath bubbles up to the
surface.

Parks have their seasons which they wear like decor-
ations. Summer grass resembles a poor man's golf course.
Spring grass is lush and edible. Winter grass is soggy, but
pleasant between the toes.

But all grass is grass. Park grass has "bouquet". Man
carves ugly graffiti on ancient monuments. We don't. We
leave a discreet reminder of having been there. We write
on grass, so to speak. And any perceptive dog can read
park grass and learn a lot.

Kensington park is the hub of my universe because we
own it, and use it more or less as we please.

By "we", I mean my canine companions, all of them
dogs of interesting background, with a role to play in
society. Domie, a Dalmatian, has something to do with

the Law. Juno, an Alsatian, speaks both German and French. Pepys, a mongrel but well schooled, is in banking and in oil. There are three Jack Russells with private income. Poodles Louis and James are in catering. They caused a scandal when they slipped through the railings and went after rabbits under Princess Margaret's windows. They were arrested and held with common criminals until released on bail.

Tinker, a fat Labrador, has South African connections. Chicot, a black poodle, is nicknamed MI5 – don't ask me why. Todd, a French boxer, lives with diplomats and eats what they eat, namely such delicacies as quiche Lorraine. Toby, an American spaniel, rides in an Embassy Cadillac.

I, McMuck, earn my living the hard way, at the typewriter.

Toby – an American spaniel – rides in an Embassy Cadillac

There are many other parks, some of them so huge you could never find your way out if lost. Hyde Park is nice but not as exclusive and intimate as Kensington. Dogs there are acquaintances rather than friends. Owners more distant. But Hyde Park attracts tourists from abroad, lonely people in need of togetherness. Togetherness is a Cavalier speciality.

St. James's Park was the one place in London where Cavaliers, and only Cavaliers, were allowed off the lead. Unfortunately the Royal Edict making this possible was rescinded. Cavaliers have lost their inalienable right. So we were told by a uniformed attendant with the bearing of a Sepoy Subahdar.

Regent's Park? Too many crossroads and restricted zones where gardeners plant and uproot and give rose-bushes short haircuts. Rowdy footballers. Mediocre Shakespeare behind the leafy walls. And the Zoological Gardens, closed to dogs. One can only imagine what goes on beyond these fences and artificial mountains.

Since I mentioned Shakespeare, I must quote one of his best lines, from *The Tempest*:

"Hawke, hawke! Bowgh-wowgh. The watch-dogges bark: Bowgh-wowgh."

Holland Park. For the birds. Literally. I mean peacocks and Siamese hens with pretentious hairdos. Dogs allowed off the lead only on lateral avenues. Some elegant setters from Campden Hill, though.

Far, far away, almost inaccessible on foot, Kenwood Park, where we go when *He* deigns to take us there by car. A fine place. Miles of hills and valleys.

A remarkable sight at Kenwood, inside Iveagh House – and you can see it if you peer through the French windows on the South side – is the portrait by Gainsborough of Lady Brisco. I say remarkable because a King Charles Cavalier stands on his hind legs, his paws in her hand. There are trees in the background, and a brook.

Now if you look closely, you will find that the Cavalier's tail is much shorter than it should be. And, on Milady's head, there is a white plume that looks exactly like a Cavalier's tail.

Amputation to satisfy the exigencies of fashion? Perish the thought!

Food and the Cavalier

> "Compose yourself. Bumble, and answer me distinctly. Do I understand that he asked for more, after he had eaten the supper allowed by the dietary?"
>
> "He did, Sir," replied Bumble.
>
> "That boy will be hung," said the gentleman in the white waistcoat, "I know that boy will be hung."
>
> CHARLES DICKENS – *Oliver Twist*

Foodliness is next to Godliness.

It is not absolutely accurate to say that the English do not pay all the attention they should to food. We dogs can't complain. Our people will cook fresh food for us and eat out of tins.

Top Dogs were spoiled by kings. Ours is an expensive diet. It was prescribed by my Veterinarian. "Breasts of chicken, and nothing else," he said, "these are white-meat dogs."

I don't mind a little veal now and then. But chicken is what I get.

When *He* heard of my menu for the following fifteen years or so my bread-winner exclaimed: "I'll feed that crazy dog chicken breasts the day the British Museum returns the Elgin marbles." Personally I don't see the connection.

So far I have consumed 2,520 chicken breasts and the world is still going around the sun . . . or vice versa.

Some do-gooders, gurus of the dog realm, tell dog lovers that there are basic rules about dog-feeding. I am always suspicious about basic rules and theology. But here is an example:

> "Pandering to a dog will not pay dividends, and there is a wealth of difference in firm but gentle handling and over-devoted giving-in."

[31]

How can there be over-devotion between man and dog?

The man in my house suggested that rabbit was white meat, and cheaper than chicken. Did he ever try to catch a rabbit? Can't be done. I have tried and failed many times in Ireland.

When a puppy takes over a home he must teach *Her* how to cook for a dog. *She* has been watching too much television with its exhibitionist dogs panting before *something* gelatinous extracted from a tin. The equivalent of man's TV dinner.

The Cavalier's lunch has to simmer on a low flame (with rice and fresh beans) until the chicken breasts are done and can be separated from the bone and diced. Overcooked, it loses much of its flavour.

Even an Englishwoman can do pretty well at the stove when coached by a difficult pet. The trouble is that their men eat trash.

Of course my ancestors had neither tins nor packaged foods. They had servants. We ate *at* not under the royal table, most often out of the royal hand. The best morsels were selected for us and courtiers drooled with envy.

Today, we Cavaliers still know the meaning of the word "service". In this egalitarian age we should be at the table. We have had to make concessions. We don't beg. We hint. An expectant look will bring down some offering, to be taken delicately, nibbled at, as if we had all the time in the world. Cavaliers don't grab.

From the dinner table come all the *bonuses*: smoked salmon, cocktail nuts, mint chocolates, Swiss cheese, smoked mackerel, *médaillon de veau*, caviare.

There are no dog cook books. Nor is there a Michelin for dogs. Oversights, surely. My French friends tell me dogs are allowed in Paris restaurants. For health reasons Anglo-Saxons keep dogs out of eating places and children out of pubs. No logical explanation.

I can't speak with authority about *Nouvelle Cuisine* or

The closest I come to gourmet French dishes is outside Chelsea
restaurants . . .

Cuisine Minceur because our English laws make it impos-
sible for me to spend holidays in France without a six-
month stay in quarantine. This Gulag for dogs is a way to
keep out rabid Latins, Goths or Vikings but it does affect
us Britons as well. It encourages our insular tendencies,
but keeps our breeding pure.

The closest I ever come to gourmet French dishes is inspecting garbage cans outside Chelsea restaurants.

The Americans, probably the most inventive of all races, get doggy-bags from head waiters at restaurants. The English are either too proud or too shy to collect remnants for home consumption. It hurts to think of the

I knew the butcher, a man of considerable charm

wealth of wasted resources left behind in eating places. All that *Canard à l'Orange*, all the *Filets Mignons*!

At one time all food came from a large pink building in London's Brompton Road. *She* did much of her buying there and I was a faithful customer. It was an institution more than a department store. I knew everyone, but my closest friend was the butcher, a man of considerable charm and expertise. I was allowed everywhere. I relished the strong aroma of smoked haddock and ripe melon. But new rules came into effect.

Today the only place open to me at Harrods is the kennel where, for many years, I have had an upper berth from which I watch the comings and goings of lesser breeds. I miss the fun of the long walks through the food halls.

I often wish I had been born 150 years ago when Englishmen still had a gargantuan appetite and tables "groaned" under the weight of meats, poultry and fish. Oh! to be under such a table near Dr. Johnson whose favourite dainties were, I am told, "A leg of pork boiled till it dropped from the bone, a veal pie with plums and sugar, and the outside of a salt buttock of beef." The good doctor used to pour the entire contents of the *butter boat*, of lobster sauce, on his plum pudding.

English eating habits surprise foreigners who tend to think that the less said about the subject the better. I have no views on the quality of the fare. What I want to know is what happened to the hearty meal.

My rare encounters with exotic foods have resulted in digestive disturbances. Friendly Texan neighbours have served me this dragon-fuel they call *chili con carne*. The after-effects are extraordinary.

I must mention, among the more unsatisfactory experiences of my under-the-table career the time spent at a lunchtime theatre where *He* took me one day. West End wags referred to it as the *munchtime* theatre . . .

We never went back and I believe it is now extinct.

The play was *Keep out; Love in Progress* by Walter Hall, a member of the cast of four. It was a mélange of suspense, comedy and sadism, inspired by a particularly shocking murder. Each member of the audience was given a fifty pence box lunch. I didn't think much of the lines but I jotted down my impressions as scraps fell under the seat:

I am a man of strange passions! Bits of tongue sandwich with watercress.

Have you come to murder me? Chunk of tinned salmon.

I had time to think . . . to brood. Slice of cucumber.

You like my bear hugs, my harsh kisses. Half a banana sandwich.

The chocolate wafer came down just when the villain was strangling his wife. That's when we left. If only it had been a Samuel Johnson production, with the accompaniment of boiled pork dropping from the bone!

Some people seem to think that it is in bad taste for a Top Dog to devote so much space to food. I have been called greedy and self-indulgent. And yet when I look around as I walk down Piccadilly I see a great many obese people and very few obese dogs. I conclude that we do not take food away from humans.

He is opposed to sybaritism in man and dog. In his youth, he says, dogs ate what they were given and they lived out in the fresh air, in dog houses. I find reminiscences about the good old days cloying. Never heard of Cavaliers in dog houses. Or dog houses in palaces.

The dog lives the life of his owners. Visitors to England should not find it surprising if, during a business meeting, a prolonged yawn followed by scratching rises from under the bank manager's desk.

So long as this form of sharing exists, no English dog need fear starvation. Even in times of adversity or shortages, the old gentleman living with his canine alter-ego in a dark bed-sitter will share his food. When nothing remains, he dies first, mourned by the faithful companion. This explains the statues in English churches of knights and ladies made of stone and stiffened for eternity, feet propped up against the flanks of splendid hounds.

History does not lie . . . even when it lies in state.

Knights and ladies made of stone, feet propped up against the flanks of splendid hounds

My Doctor and I

"I am the dog: no, the dog is himself and I am the
dog, – O the dog is me and I am myself; ay, so, so . . ."
Two Gentlemen of Verona

Englishmen don't talk about their health. They cringe at
the thought of a "personal" remark. But give them free
rein on the subject of dog health and they cannot be
stopped.

Dog parents, especially those of Cavaliers, need constant reassurance. They feel their pet's pain more than he
does. A good Veterinary Surgeon takes a close look at the
sick animal but an even closer look at the owner. This is
known as Psychosomatic Medicine. The idea is that if you
take care of human anxieties, the body of dog or cat
responds.

A few words, then, about the Vet, the most important
creature after the butcher. I am a regular patient, have
been since puppyhood. The surgery of Mr. B. is situated
at the end of a Mews. It has an operating room at the back
and a hospital upstairs with several "beds".

There is no National Health scheme for dogs in Britain
but it is bound to come some day.

There are two ways of dealing with dog ailments: too
early or too late. Some people never bother to detect early
symptoms and bring the patient to the Vet too late.
Others see symptoms everywhere and spend their life in
the surgery. Between these extremes there is nothing. No
grey area.

Mr. B.'s waiting-room is always full. Long before they
are summoned in for examination the dogs begin to
shiver. Shivers are contagious and uncontrollable. The
women in the waiting-room put on a brave face, as women
will, and indulge in idle talk about worming, cute habits,
dog's superiority over husband or lover.

[38]

One reason for my frequent trips to the Vet is my trouble with musc glands. These have been inherited by Cavaliers from a distant ancestor, the fox. Musc glands get clogged and have to be looked after. Sorry to mention this humiliating condition, but this is *entre nous*. Musc glands are located under the tail.

The man in my house is not sympathetic. When informed of the Cavalier's need for this form of maintenance *He* looked up "Fox" in his *Britannica* and, having found what he wanted, he shouted: "I knew it! McMuck descends from Reynard. He is a transvestite fox! Tally Ho! Foxes have glands under the tail and so has McMuck."

That the man should be ignorant of the important difference between caudal glands and anal glands doesn't surprise me. I do resent his references to "Bottom Dog", however.

I have an impressive pharmacy. My remedies are stored in the guest bathrooms. This way if mistakes occur they can only inconvenience a few friends spending the weekend.

The following list of health requisites tells its own story:

Dog Medicine Chest	*Man's Medicine Chest*
Multi-vitamins	Phensic
Digitalis	Alka Seltzer
Butazolidine	Milk of Magnesia
Panine for indigestion	
Tranquillizers	
Flea powder (optional)	
Sleeping pills	
Ear drops	
Optrex eye pads	
Ointment for cuts	
Talcum powder	
Baby lotion	
Skin cream	

My private Veterinarian is a born diplomat, of the stick-and-carrot generation. When I am on *the table* for an injection or worse, he keeps one hand around my neck. The other, containing chocolate drops, is under my nose. We have an understanding.

Why is it that we cherish our tormentors? By nature I am a growler. I snap at the hand that brushes me, but never at the hand that feeds me.

The English Vet can be reached at any time of the day or night, even on Sundays. He makes phone calls. The physician could learn from him. It was not always thus. For centuries Veterinarians catered only to the so-called *useful* (meaning edible) beasts: horses, pigs, cows, sheep. No attention was being paid to dog health. Finally, in 1897, the first treatises on the dog's "Management" came out in print. A Medical Dictionary on Dogs was compiled.

Until that time it had been Horse, Horse, Horse, under such absurd title as *The Exterior of the Horse* (interior obviously unworthy of mention . . . stuffed with hay) or *Common Colics of the Horse*. Can you believe it? A whole book on horse manure.

Today the Vet knows that the dog is the client of choice, whose call is heard above the din of daily routine. This is as it should be. The dog is the backbone of the Englishman's home.

At last, the dog has won recognition. The *Oxford Companion of Literature* lists twice as many famous dogs as famous horses. *Not a single famous cat*! Famous dogs had no Vets. This goes for Bill Sykes's dog "Bull's Eye" in *Oliver Twist*, for Sir Walter Scott's "Maida", for Wordsworth's "Music", for Byron's "Boatswain" who inspired these immortal lines carved on a monument:

"Beauty without Vanity, Strength without Insolence, Courage without Ferocity, and all the Virtues of Man without his Vices."

My private Veterinarian is a born diplomat . . . We have an understanding

I doubt that a Vet was called to take care of Carlyle's dog "Nero" who sprang from the library window and fell "plash" on to the pavement without a bone being broken. Later he was run over by a butcher's cart and he "died from the effects of the accident" says Virginia Woolf.

Not one of these famous dogs had their own doctor. Medical knowledge was being wasted on bovines. The mind boggles.

My doctor has told my people that Cavaliers are not renowned for their courage. They yell before they get hurt. Can anyone suggest a better way? Come to think of it, isn't this yelling before the pain the very definition of bravery; apprehension on the eve of battle followed by haughty disregard of danger in action? The preventive howl is the secret of survival. They call us Cavaliers as a tribute to our knightly forebears.

At the Vet I pay scant attention to other patients. What ails them is their business. I do not sympathize with the trembling grey poodle in the crimson overcoat, or the miniature collie with the stupid expression, or the scared spaniel who swallowed a toy sailboat's anchor.

I always say that in this world it is Man eat Man, and Every Dog for Himself.

McMuck on People

"And then to walk in St. James's Park, and saw a great variety of fowl which I never saw before."

Diary of Samuel Pepys – LORD'S DAY 1661

By now the reader will have gathered that I live in a typical English household where whatever I say goes and most of what I do is not only tolerated, but praised.

But I must confess that, in England, what one sees and hears does not always make sense. Take the way Londoners have modified their appearance over the years. The public at the Changing of the Guard, in the parks, looks stranger every day.

I enjoy a walk across St. James's Park now and then. Nostalgia perhaps? Every time I walk there my mind wanders back to that fateful day, 30 January 1649, at 10 am, when the King stepped on to the scaffold at Whitehall and caught a last glimpse of the Palace where his body would soon be brought in a coffin draped in black velvet.

The scene is very present, very real. I don't know if

Most of what I do is tolerated . . .

others see it as clearly as I do. The people I meet on these commemorative outings get smaller every day, more sallow in complexion. Even the shape of the eyes is different. These Londoners bristle with cameras.

I am told that these are not, as I surmised, Englishmen affected by ecological phenomena, but travellers who have come from distant lands across the seas to pay homage to my late monarch. I can hardly believe it, yet it could be true.

In recent years the veil, the sari, the kimono have become fashionable London garb. In Kensington Gardens I often meet groups of women strolling under the chestnut trees attired in tent-like clothing. Their merry chatter gives way to shrill cries if a dog comes too near. I cannot believe that under these many yards of black material there beats the heart of a dog-loving Englishwoman.

London smells are different. On the street where I live, the aroma of the Sunday roast has given way to more exotic perfumes. Sitting on my balcony I can hear Armenian choirs from the church across the way. Two floors above, Nigerian millionaires play their reggae tapes. From Flat No. 40 rises the smell of gigot d'agneau, and from No. 37, that of sauerkraut.

The whole of the Royal Borough is impregnated with the unmistakable signature of MacDonald's hamburgers. Here and there one discerns the perfumes of Arabia, incense from India, marijuana from the London School of Economics.

In this symphony of odours, as I sniff, I realize we have achieved at last the ideals of One World which inspired the founders of the United Nations.

Dogs differ from other dogs "externally". Human differences go deeper. I often try and understand what separates an Englishman from an American. Not easy. Some of my best friends are Americans. Superficially, they could be carbon copies of the English. Yet the similarities are only skin-deep.

Americans like heat and cold. They sweat in winter and freeze in summer. Something to do with thermostats. Englishmen are uncomfortable all year round. Americans, I have found, store food in tins and boxes and refrigerators. Some of it doesn't smell like food at all. They keep things like peanut butter, ice cream, hominy grits. They fry chicken and they pop corn. They make pies out of practically anything, including pumpkin and pecans. These are customs handed down by settlers.

The English and American tribes speak approximately the same language but the English say "Luvverly day" at the first drops of rain, and the Americans say "Have a nice day" when night falls.

The English are not *au courant* with the latest Paris fashions, but they know which horses will win races. Americans assume all dogs are healthy (hence the expression "Lucky Dog") but they keep worrying about their own state of health.

Also, there is this complicated business about "he", "she" and "it".

As far as I can tell, the English recognize two genders: masculine and feminine, just as we do in the canine world. The third group, the marginals, is not considered important.

The Americans have developed such an intense dislike of genders that words like *man* and *woman* must be avoided. Gentlemen become gentlepersons. A lady chairman is a chairperson, a piece of furniture.

All this happened quite recently, in my short lifetime. America saw fit to impose on the rest of the world (which paid no attention) the abbreviated title of Ms, a compromise between Mrs. and Miss. The United Nations adopted that (designation) probably to keep Unopigs in their place. The European Commission did not. By the time

Ms crossed the Atlantic it had a faint ring of mockery.

Dogs don't accept neutering. We insist on genders. The original male chauvinist pig, the Emperor Fu-hi of China, who introduced matrimony three thousand years ago, prescribed that *All good things are male, the less good ones female*. It is from Fu-hi that we inherited genders. We haven't been quite sure what to do with it. In the animal kingdom the strong were meant to be males, the weak, females. But there is always an animal weaker than the weak. Therefore, foxes (feminine) destroyed masculine chickens, and masculine mice were caught by feminine cats.

The French, eminently practical people, don't have neuters. The British don't want to know. The Germans want to know too much, hence the confusion. A German *Maedchen* or *Fraulein* is neutral. So is the chauvinist *Schwein*.

I am only saying all this in passing, to make a point.

All dogs remain dogs. Top Dogs more so. People can become foreigners. Dogs don't.

Americans travelling abroad are immersed in foreigners. The English staying at home are in the same predicament. All very confusing. Must make head or tail of it.

Every summer I see millions of Americans who have become foreigners and who don't know it. The English, wherever they go outside their own country, remain foreigners and enjoy the experience.

Dogs hate to leave home unless home grows wheels and becomes a caravan and the whole family goes along.

People who travel think they save money by taking cheap flights, then they discover that hotel bills and restaurant meals have been boosted to make up the difference. Swings and roundabouts, as we English say.

I can tell Amercians on the street early in the morning because they are the only people there. They don't know that, in London, it doesn't pay to be the early bird unless you are looking for worms. At 7 am I meet freshly laundered Yanks walking aimlessly through the streets when the only thing alive around them is the garbage.

Italians, they tell me, speak sign language. But you must be careful about finger gestures. Winston Churchill made excellent use of the V (for victory) sign. Don't try it with the fingers together, though.

Behind every great statesman lies a faithful dog

Englishmen travel with luggage inherited from Edwardian aunts. Americans carry their clothes in nylon covers. They look like kidnappers when they land in Europe, lugging these corpse-like carriers.

What else do I know about Englishmen and Americans?

The English go to America to lose weight. To accomplish this they wear so-called light-weight suits in eighty degree heat. The Americans come to London to get dressed like Englishmen. But the first question anyone ever asks when they appear in their new Savile Row suit is, "How are things in Tacoma?"

We dogs judge people by their shoes. In a single day we see hundreds of types and sizes at very close range. I have noticed that the English wear expensive shoes that are not shined, whereas most Americans have shoes of lesser quality that sparkle under layers of expensive creams and polishes.

What else have I learned about people?

The American sees the world (through television) in colour. The English are colour blind because receivers cost too much. Personally I can't tell the difference.

Such are my thoughts about people. Do people deserve all the attention dogs pay them? I don't know. As a Londoner I think the human population of London grows too fast. I don't see that proliferation improves my city.

One good thing, though. Londoners have kept their trees growing in the streets. London trees get taller as Londoners stay man-sized, and the London dog, dog-sized.

We dogs judge people by their shoes

Cavalier Views on the Animal Kingdom

"Some animals have only a limited education, and use only very simple words, and scarcely ever a comparison or a flowery figure; whereas certain other animals have a large vocabulary, a fine command of language and a ready and fluent delivery."

MARK TWAIN – *A Tramp Abroad*

The national language of dogs is English. Or so, at least, think the British who invented it.

Actually, dogs are the only creatures who understand *all* languages and who, among themselves, speak a common tongue, a form of esperanto.

The people in my house went abroad for a few days, leaving me in the care of a family of French diplomats. Whenever my hosts addressed me they did so in English. Speaking to each other they reverted to French. I understood every word of course.

I think the English have a special relationship with animals, and yet are unaware of much that goes on in our world. They *think* they know.

Not that the media can be accused of laxity when it comes to animals in the news. Every time a mawkishly sentimental dog photo lands on the editor's desk he plasters the front page with it. Canine cheesecake. Brings tears to the driest of eyes. Sells papers.

But watch these same hacks join the hue and cry against dogs versus pavement! They do whip up the Londoner's hostility towards my kind.

Year after year the campaign against dogs grows in intensity. But too little attention is paid to brave deeds of dogs mobilized against crime, as drug detectors, or guardians of the national heritage.

[49]

In 1961 a Goya painting worth hundreds of thousands of pounds was stolen in broad daylight from the National Gallery. Security had to be tightened. Who was entrusted with sentry duty at night? The faithful and reliable German shepherd, of course. London wags said then that a retriever would have been more useful.

The disappearance of Wellington's portrait by Goya made a deep impression on museum directors. Dogs took over from man. They were brought in through the back door and received too little publicity. They guarded the collection of French masterpieces loaned to the Arts Council. Private galleries also turned to dogs to prevent thefts. By day, human guards took over. It was assumed, wrongly I believe, that dogs would not be able to tell art lovers from thieves.

As crime increases, man must rely on dogs to curb it. But who protects dogs against discrimination?

Dogs' rights were not mentioned at the conferences in Helsinki or Belgrade. The right of a dog to stay under his master's table in a restaurant is denied in Britain but fully recognized in Paris or Vienna. Travel guides still use as a symbol of *No Dogs Allowed* the head of a hound with crossed lines superimposed. The sign of infamy.

American dogs, I hear, enjoy greater freedom than English or European dogs. Roaming is their right. It is encouraged by an absence of fences, by lawns that invite trespassing. This *Don't Fence Me In* attitude is in sharp contrast with Europe's addiction to walls and hedgerows.

Americans, however, still tolerate the shady character, politically motivated, who goes under the name of Dog Warden. Alas the dog-catcher is making his debut in Britain where 50 local authorities out of 369 have hired one.

The report of the "Working Party on Dogs" published in 1976 urged the adoption of a dog warden scheme. This report made little impact on suburban and country

Dogs guarded the collection of French masterpieces

districts where dogs are still free to roam as long as they leave sheep alone.

Accused of laxity in dog control, the Kennel Club (my Club incidentally) countered with attacks on dog owners who give their pets too much freedom. A Club statement attributed anti-dog sentiment in a nation of dog worshippers to "strays roaming around, mating indiscriminately, forming packs".

Now where do you think these roamers got their ideas from? In South Kensington, my borough, there is much indiscriminate mating in packs among humans in flats and bed-sits. Nobody suggests a *Working Party on Man*.

The offensive against dogs started in England in January 1978 with articles that unleashed a wave of letters to the editors. Dog haters were outnumbered by dog lovers. The debate goes on. Its general conclusion is that owners, rather than dogs, need educating. I say amen to this. We Cavaliers have always been willing to learn. And people have learned from us. Remember the entry in Samuel Pepys' Diary for 11 September 1661, concerning Dr. Williams's dog who killed all the cats attacking the doctor's pigeons and buried them:

> "And if the tip of the tail hangs out he will take up the cat again and dig the hole deeper, which is very strange."

The anti-dog movement in the British Isles threatens to divide families. There are angry orange-coloured notices in the ground-floor windows of patrician London houses, asking dog-walkers to be as considerate towards humans as they are towards dogs. Some of us must go about our business stealthily, as if afraid of being accused of soliciting.

If class barriers rise again as a result of legislation against dogs, there is no telling what counter-revolutions will be plotted in the kennels of England. Public opinion will be with us. Dog lovers are more prolific writers than dog haters.

The Lord be praised for the rebirth of *The Times*, a newspaper which, in one of its leaders, recognized that "Dogs and their masters deserve wide toleration and a pretty free run".

Still, anything concerning dogs leaves its mark on the public mind. The people are conscious of the dog's role as communicator, security blanket and marriage counsellor.

The people who walk us need us more than ever now that they have caught the American disease of jogging. Britons no longer walk their dogs around monuments to Queen Victoria, they run. Dogs run along, exhorting them, providing the much needed stimulus and inspiration.

Finally, I was delighted to see the Post Office issue of stamps bearing the likenesses of four favourite British dogs and Her Majesty's profile on each one of the stamps. What other country would acknowledge officially the role of dogdom in the Kingdom?

So much for my clan.

Other animals compete for a share of the limelight. Some succeed.

Peers in stately homes have lions. Vintage cars didn't suffice to draw the crowds.

In the House of Commons a six-hour debate on the behaviour of bulls in pastures frequented by hikers resulted in sharp exchanges between Members who said that bulls are not dangerous when out with cows, and those who insisted that "Many people who go into the countryside cannot tell the difference between a bull and a bullock".

A compromise was reached at last, in the traditional English way, whereby bulls were to accept a voluntary code of conduct, being allowed freedom to romp at certain times, on given days.

Now and again giraffes, pythons and eagles are the talk of the town. Do they really deserve all that space and time in papers and on TV? They rely on showmanship, and curiosity value.

The giraffe over-extended himself during an amorous encounter, did a ballet split and failed to get up. For days, until his death, he monopolized the headlines.

Lady Kimber's python, a seven-foot animal named "Thag", was missing from her cage in Fulham. To reassure the public, an Assistant Curator of Reptiles at the London Zoo said the python was not yet long enough to strangle a human being: "At the moment it couldn't even eat a newborn baby, but it could give you a good nip." Eventually the python was found basking in the sun in a bed of geraniums.

Goldie, the London Zoo eagle, broke out of his prison some years ago and went rabbit-hunting on the lawns surrounding the residence of the American Ambassador in Regent's Park. What better place for an eagle?

Goldie's picture adorned every newspaper every day for more than a week. Despite the bitter cold, thousands of Londoners turned bird-watchers. Taped mating calls made no impression on the fugitive. It was suggested that the Ambassador, the Hon. David K. E. Bruce, would need special protection. He declined, pointing out that his two large springer spaniels were quite capable of dealing with Goldie . . . if they ever woke up. In the end, the eagle's carnivorous instincts brought him back to his cage, generously stocked with raw meat. A bargain basement philosopher remarked that if there was anything sadder than a caged eagle it was an eagle that did not know what to do with his freedom.

Goldie slipped up when he attacked a dog, inspiring this comment in a leader: "Noble eagle versus man's best friend – that was the dilemma confronting Britain . . ."

The English dog retains his rank among animals of historical importance. Walk around Westminster Abbey and see who lies at the feet of the Kings, Queens, Princes and Bishops entombed there. Mostly dogs.

Some beasts in the Abbey one would not be seen dead with. Imagine Lady Frances, Countess of Sussex, feet propped up against a porcupine! A French custom, they tell me. I wouldn't be surprised! Anything for a thrill.

Top Dog on the Working Dog

"We have good reason to believe that England has long been famous for dogs, which, on the authority of Strabo, were much sought after by all the surrounding nations".

NIMROD – *The Horse and Hound*, 1843

I have never heard of a Cavalier King Charles spaniel who accepted to work for a living. The notion of the "working dog" is abhorrent. And yet other breeds allow themselves to be used by man.

The over-zealous sheepdog showing off at trials pretends to be on the side of law and order when, in fact, he would enjoy nothing more than a raw hind quarter of lamb. But the ignorant masses are fooled by these collies even if I am not.

Police dogs, like the military, are masters rather than servants, and I am not including them among dogs who hire themselves out or who are in "trade". Seeing-eye dogs guiding the blind deserve our gratitude. Beyond this point I draw the line.

I am deeply suspicious of the motives of enormous St. Bernards who roam the Alps in search of allegedly "lost" mountaineers. Their holier-than-thou look, their piety, don't fool me. They are, indeed, fostering alcoholism and their activities should be investigated. I have no time for mercenary Swiss dogs who pull carts loaded with milk churns.

I have heard of males who sell their charms. Professional siring may be an enjoyable profession but, in my opinion, debasing. Anyway, I am sure these are "jobs for the boys", jobs available only to dogs with pull, something to do with the old school tie.

The English have invested sports that require the help of dogs. Top Dogs participate only as spectators.

St. Bernards are fostering alcoholism

Best known of the sporting dogs are the hounds and the beagles who, like human joggers, will run for hours to prove to themselves that it can be done. If a-hunting we must go, is it not more noble to hunt alone than in a pack, giving tongue, playing games prescribed by the "unspeakable" chasing the "uneatable", as the fox-hunter and his prey have been described?

For my part I have always avoided the early morning "meet" when the frost is on the ground. When I join, my favourite observation post is the back seat of a heated car, beside the hamper of food and drink. But it is all a matter of taste and I know that the qualities of British dogs were fully appreciated by the Romans who appointed a high functionary whose mission was to collect and breed recruits for the arenas of Rome and for the Emperor's kennels.

Man has learned how to live with idle dogs. It has taken a long time. Not very long ago we were still being treated like second-class citizens.

My blood boils when I am told that a certain Major-General W. N. Hutchinson, *Late Colonel Grenadier Guards*, wrote an entire opus on the subject of *Dog Breaking*. I must quote from this disgraceful treatise if only to prove that no one in his right mind would dare express himself in this manner today. The R.S.P.C.A. would take immediate action. There would be hundreds of letters to *The Times*.

Judge for yourselves, and bear in mind that the Colonel's style of writing is as insufferable as his attitude. Listen, for instance, to the typical male chauvinist pig:

"It is to be observed that ladies' dogs are generally so pampered and overfed that a common reward does not stimulate them to exertion to the same degree it does dogs less favoured ... The fair sex, though possessing unbounded and most *proper* influence over us, notoriously have but little control over their canine favourites ... Hear ye, ladies who would be glad that your pretty pets were a hundreds times more obedient than you find them."

Now who does the Major-General think he is? And he goes on in this way for pages leading to the conclusion that ladies "cannot teach a four-footed pet any tricks beyond the art of begging".

This was written in 1865. It could have been the Middle

Ages, especially when we come to the burning subject of corporal punishment.

The author of *Dog Breaking* (a revolting expression anyway) is for caning, naturally. He calls it *chastising*:

> "Pause between each cut (of the whip) and so that he may comprehend why he is punished, call out several times, but not loudly, 'Toho-bad-toho', and crack your whip . . . When the chastisement is over, stand in front of him and prevent his thinking of bolting . . ."

If this method of communication were not so repulsive I would call it absurd. But such was the style and demeanour of the Victorian *macho*, all brawn and no brain, who reveals the extent of his prejudices when he concludes:

> "So long as you are a bachelor, you can make a companion of your dog without incurring the danger of his being spoiled by your wife and children."

Who is it, I wonder, who called it "the good old days"?

Sweet moments in a short life

Top Dog's Dog-days

> "The days about the time of the heliacal rising of the Dog-Star are known as Dog-days (3 July to 11 August) . . . due to the belief that at this season dogs are most apt to run mad."

> *Oxford Companion of English Literature*

We have all heard about mad dogs and Englishmen – that slur put to music. Why do the British want us to share their madness? A convenient way, I suppose, for them to look saner.

Still, I must agree that there is such a thing as summer madness. For most people it is just the "silly season", when grown-ups have a last fling before schools release their inmates and when hordes of unleashed, dishevelled younger creatures pour out of scruffy provincial trains to reclaim their territory.

For the English dog this time of the year brings with it upheavals and changes in lifestyles. Social life excludes most of us. You don't see many wolfhounds at Ascot or at garden parties. Not for the likes of us the popping champagne corks, the after-theatre dinners at the Savoy Grill, the tête-à-tête at Annabelle's. In the country we are tolerated, but the great weekend house-parties of yore are few and far between, and, anyway, we were never popular on the croquet lawns of England.

But in all these yesterdays that will never return we did have our retinue of faithful domestics. They knew how to keep us well fed and entertained in that self-contained paradise, the kitchen area, where the lovely smell of hot gooseberry pies blended so well with that of floor polish. Where are they now, our retainers?

Today, when the people of the house want their freedom they telephone the dog-sitter. And almost always tragedy strikes when the dog-sitter moves in or we move out with the dog-sitter.

As a rule, dog-sitters are young ladies in tight jeans, in love with pop singers. Young ladies who brush or comb their hair while watching television instead of brushing or combing ours. Who tell us what is good for us, namely interminable walks in the rain with other dogs – all on the lead – like the prison yard round.

The dog-sitter does for money what our human best friends do out of love or a sense of duty. They are hired to keep us company, on the assumption that they fill the appalling void left by the migratory family.

During the "season" the dog-sitter is summoned several times a week. And the "season" (not to be confused with the time of the year when dogs get lovesick) coincides roughly with dog-days of madness and frustration. Responsibilities are dumped into the lap of the dog-sitter. If things go wrong during the temporary stewardship the dog-sitter is accountable. And so, naturally, we do our best to make things happen which would never happen otherwise. It gives one a great feeling of satisfaction to greet the returning people with a hang-dog expression, a slow wave of the tail, and a foot in a plaster cast.

In the happy old days normal people holidayed on the Isle of Wight and dogs went along. Now there is this mania of the complete change of scenery and the holiday abroad among strangers on oil-soaked beaches where nudism blooms.

The warning comes with the packing of the bags and the loading of the car with all the paraphernalia needed to turn man into fish (whence he came). For us it marks the beginning of dog-days. Enter the dog-sitter. These social workers prefer the company of dogs to that of parents, whereas most dogs are happier with people than with other dogs. There can be no meeting of minds.

The dog-sitter may be called in for a few hours during the day or evening, when the woman of the house plays bridge or when a dinner party serves as an excuse. Short absences of this kind are tolerable. But the long succession of dog-days in summer, without one's normal entourage, is more than one can endure.

I know that the kennel is worse by far, but I am not discussing prison life.

You can tell at a glance when a dog is out with the dog-sitter. He walks behind her like a robot, tail down, head down. And if she happens to have a boy-friend she

The dog-sitter

will spend long hours with him on a park bench or lying in the grass. What I know about birds and bees I have learned from dog-sitters like Sylvia, a very presentable red-head who used to tie my lead to her ankle while wrestling amorously with Carlos, the Berlitz pupil from Guatemala.

What I know about pub life I have learned from Amanda, who took me to the Britannia every evening. Pubs are fun, but for short periods. Very few Englishmen can drink sitting down, so all a dog sees in a pub are feet. Amanda's local came close to winning the "Pub of the Year" contest. What criteria are applied in such a selection remains a mystery to me. I understand that the publican's personality, the way he handles draught beer, the decor, have something to do with it.

A distinguished pub-crawler, columnist Angus McGill, once wrote: "We don't view too kindly the 17th Century pub with the jukebox, or the ultra-modern bar with antiques. Some landlords put so much chintz about that you can't find your way to the Gents." The latter doesn't bother me, nor did it seem to bother dog-sitter Amanda. But the jukebox was a pain.

Dog-sitter Alexis (twice-bitten, never shy) allowed poodles Louis and James to romp to Holland Park, off the lead. They pounced on a peacock and did him in. The fine was £100 – ridiculously high when you think that you can buy a peacock for £7.50 down in Kent. This shows how blind Justice can be when dogs get into trouble. Was it not Thomas Hood who asked: "For what is Law, unless Poor Dogs can get it . . . Dog cheap?"

Dog-sitter Heather was mad about horses. I had to run behind her while she galloped in Hyde Park and the only kick I got out of it was the one that required eight stitches under the jaw. Dog-sitter Heather has never been forgiven for using me to pay for her riding lessons. She emigrated to Tasmania.

Dog-sitter Marylin, a drop-out from Brighton Poly-technic, was entrusted with the care of a ten-month-old St. Bernard who killed himself jumping out of a first-floor window when he saw the South Kensington refuse-tip go by.

Without dog-sitters, London in summer is not an unpleasant place. It is no longer considered vulgar to stay in town at weekends if you don't have a country estate. In fact people will credit you with sanity if you fail to join the steaming masses on the highways, down to the sea or up to the hills. Even outdoor life in the parks is colourful when you are with your own kind, the regular residents of your house. Indian families squat under the elms, the mothers well wrapped in their saris, the men stripped to the waist. In St. James's Park the sun worshippers who have escaped from government offices expose a minimum of chicken-white flesh to the heat.

In Regent's Park you come across couples walking slowly, conversing in German. The Russians prefer Kew Gardens or Highgate. The Americans play softball in Hyde Park with tribal zeal, filling the air with whoops and screams.

Traffic flows more normally in summer. Tourists take the low road to the Tower or the high road to Madame Tussaud's, and some of them are never seen again. Tele-phones don't ring. No one expects anyone to be in town. No bills are sent out.

But the dog on loan to the dog-sitter pines in the darkest recesses of the pub, reflecting on the drinking habits of the English so aptly described many years ago in the London *Times*:

"A dash of hypocrisy, a modicum of permissiveness, and a splash of sincere anxiety, topped off with a large helping of inconsistency."

[63]

Top Dog in Top Gear

"Oh! to drive in England, now that spring is there"

ROBERT BROWNING (I think)

The motor-car is one of the rare inventions of modern man that is of use to dogs. Therefore, dogs make full use of the car, and Top Dogs prefer top cars.

The English have been making motorcars for donkeys' years. Manufacturers never fail to feature man's best friend in their advertising, sitting or standing beside the shooting brake with couple in well-tailored tweeds.

Children get car-sick all the time. Dogs don't . . . well hardly ever. This makes the dog the ideal travelling companion on the road, and a very observant one. The dog is interested in what he sees, the child is bored.

The best observation post for the driving dog is right behind the man or woman at the wheel, with paws on the driver's back-rest or, preferably, on his or her shoulder. This gives one excellent visibility and car control. It is a comfortable position for a snooze, and no one seems to mind a little slobbering or slavering.

Some car owners erect a barrier between themselves and their dogs, unaware of the deep psychological wounds inflicted on the fenced-in passenger reduced to the rank of baggage. In my case, I am happy to say, there is complete togetherness with my people, even when my coat is soaked with rain and *He* says I smell like the dirty mop used for cleaning the floor of the railway station's snack bar.

If I had my choice I would drive a Rolls-Royce. My people do not own one. A pity. Having had an opportunity to ride in one once or twice with a chauffeur friend who works for a gentleman from Abu Dhabi, I regard it as a vehicle of class even though some models are named after French swamps, or styled by Italians and equipped with Japanese record players.

[64]

I understand that driving a Rolls nowadays puts you in the same social category as disc jockeys, pop singers and sheikhs – people who, one way or another, have struck oil. I don't see what is wrong with that. There is nothing like real leather and precious wood as a setting for a dog of means.

As an English Top Dog I always urge my compatriots to *Buy British* but my exhortations have been falling on deaf ears. More than half the cars on the street where I live are German, French, Swedish, Italian or Japanese. Personally I find this scandalous. But, come to think of it, dogdom is affected by the same foreign disease. There are too many poodles, dachshunds, schnauzers and Absos around for comfort. A little protectionism wouldn't hurt. I bet Enoch Powell doesn't go for this mongrelization.

Were it not for certain physical limitations imposed upon us by the Creator – in His wisdom I am sure – we dogs could teach British drivers a thing or two. After many years of backseat driving I have my own views on motoring in England.

To get out to the countryside from the big city requires, as a rule, an hour or so of crawling through a string of High Streets where pedestrians have an absolute priority. On Saturdays a constant flow of housewives and aspiring brides stream across what should be a highway. This is the day when women rush about from the stationery store where they buy "Get Well" cards to the chemist for hair curlers.

It is not that English pedestrians are anti-motorist, but they do not think the automobile is here to stay and, in a sense, they may well be right. There is an energy crisis.

At one stage of his development the pedestrian becomes a cyclist. The English cyclist, a heroic figure under normal circumstances, becomes God-like under pelting rain, when his machine shoots up water high and wide and he turns into the nautical equivalent of a Roman candle.

When about to make a turn, the cyclist extends an infinitely long arm in the approximate direction of his presumed goal. The motorist has little choice but to slam on his brakes, for nothing deters a cyclist. Women cyclists – not easily distinguishable from the male when dressed for "weather" – are even fiercer in their single-mindedness.

It is on the bicycles of Hertfordshire, not on the playing fields of Eton, that the soldiery of England develop the qualities they later display on the River Kwai or at Arnhem. As for the motorcyclists they never really make it to the battlefields. Their fate is settled on the motorway.

Motorway excitement in England is as short-lived as the motorways are short. Some motorways dot the landscape like bits of earthworms attacked by madmen wielding spades. The so-called open road is largely mythical. As soon as the driver reaches a certain speed a sign appears telling him that *Motorway Ends*. The same is true of these lovely roads known as dual "carriageways" where I always expect to hear the cracking of horsewhips.

I must say that most of my driving is on narrow country roads, my motorist being allergic to motorways and to the smell of chips from their restaurants. The two-lane winding road flanked by hedgerows, is where all thoughts of passing must be abandoned, unless the car ahead is a vintage Hispano, manned by a retired headmistress swathed in muslin veils.

Then there is the one-lane road where you play follow-the-leader behind a tractor and where the pedestrian assumes truly giant proportions. No matter whether he is the ageing botanist stalking a herbaceous perennial, or the rubber-booted herdsman on his way to fetch the cows, the pedestrian has the right of way and he pushes the motorist into a clinch with the hedges. Observe the left side of most cars and you will discern, under the spit and polish, the telltale marks of Nature's claws.

The British cyclist is a heroic figure

I have noticed that English drivers have succumbed to the lure of unisex fashions. More often than not the auburn-haired beauty at the wheel of the slow-moving Citroen 2 CV turns out to be sporting a beard when one overtakes her.

There is a love-hate relationship between man and car in which we dogs play no part. The car is here to serve us. Too often, man lives to drive instead of driving to live. When a Frenchman exclaims, "I shall never allow anyone to lay his hands on her!" he isn't speaking of his wife but of his car, the fourth member of the eternal quadrangle . . . "*la Voiture*". The Englishman's attitude towards the motor-car is more complex.

The Englishman's main concern is to avoid paying for parking or for a garage as long as possible. Most British cars are rugged outdoor types who wear a touch of rust with the insourciance of a woman made up for a fancy dress ball. They stay out of doors, gathering soot, dust, pollen and a liberal coating of pigeon guano. And then, suddenly, on Saturday or Sunday, owners appear with plastic buckets and rags, to revive the forsaken beasts. Other vehicles dissolve slowly under our very eyes, ending up like donkeys in the Mexican desert after the coyotes have feasted on the edible parts.

What you will not find in motoring magazines over here is the advertisement I read in an American publication with the catch-line: *If you are a two-car family with a one-car garage, your second car may feel rejected*. Not for the Londoner this bemoaning of the mental condition of his second car, assuming he has a second car. If his children can grow up on the soggy fields of private schools under the steady drizzle, the car can take life outside the house, without sessions at the psychoanalyst.

But there are people who pamper their car's libido by housing it in a converted stable. The mews garage is so narrow sometimes that the driver gets out of it through the roof or back door.

I understand that in America the car owner would build a second garage as an insurance against rejection. This, to me, illustrates one of the many differences between our two worlds.

Looking around me in the streets of London I am impressed by the number of vehicles that reach a venerable age despite the rough treatment they receive. It must be something in the air, as humans always say when groping for an explanation.

[68]

A Cavalier View of the Arts

"It follows not, because the hair is rough, the dog is a savage one."

SHERIDAN KNOWLES – "The Daughter"

Cavaliers – and some other dogs – have had a profound influence on language.

When man comes to a sad end he is said to have died like a dog. Of man dressed to kill we say he resembles a dog's dinner. If he expresses delight he is a dog with two tails. In his fight for survival in the business world he is compared to the dog that eats dog.

There are lucky dogs, gay dogs, dull dogs, sly dogs, sea dogs, lame dogs, bottom dogs and, of course, Top Dogs.

My French isn't what it used to be but the infiltration by dogs speaking that language has not escaped my attention. France's *chiens* are in evidence everywhere.

Of a plucky fellow we say that *Il a du chien*. The avenger keeps his bitch's pup (*Le chien de sa chienne*) for his enemy. If you are going to be bitten in French, get bitten by a dog rather than a bitch, the French say. Which means you might "As well be hung for a sheep as for a lamb".

To be received like a dog in a bowling alley (*Comme un chien dans un jeu de quilles*) becomes, in English, inexplicably, "To be as welcome as a dog at a wedding". I say inexplicably because English weddings often teem with dogs.

Cats have given us very little in the way of popular expressions and new words. But the French know how to deal with the species.

A Frenchman who hasn't time for you says, "*J'ai d'autres chats à fouetter*"; he has other cats to thrash. Or when he wishes to minimize an issue not worth bothering about he says, "*Il n'y a pas de quoi fouetter un chat*".

Rational, logical people, the French. They take it all out on the cat.

Books and the inner dog

To some dogs the love of good books comes early in life.

While I cannot speak for all King Charles Spaniels I re-member the thrill I got the first time I ventured in the library where *He* keeps his collection of rare volumes. Here, before me, was a new world, a bibliophile's paradise.

May I confess a preference for antiquarian tomes with thick backs and a brand of glue on the spine not found in most modern bindings. I spent hours, undisturbed and unnoticed, in the penumbra of the study, where the more massive books filled the lower shelves.

I nibbled at the back of a South Sea Islands saga until it was *al dente*, ready for peeling and chewing. I went through a de luxe edition of the *Odes* of John Keats (a limited printing of 120). One taste of Keats and you crave more.

A *Voyage Round the World* by Gemelli, printed in 1695, was as good as new. Succulent despite centuries of neglect. I consumed several art books, more filling and satisfying I think than history. The glossy paper may have something to do with it.

During a weekend in the country, when I was left downstairs with a deaf Labrador who cared more about horses than about our cultural heritage, I gnawed at several volumes of an American encyclopaedia of music. This took several hours, overnight. I have not been back to this particular residence since then.

One likes to share such rare pleasures with others. The sharing occurred the day the cleaning woman pushed away the sofa hiding the books in my home and screamed in a mixture of Mediterranean tongues.

My people displayed an absence of self-control which struck me as un-British. I was threatened with various forms of punishment, including the muzzle.

May I confess a preference for antiquarian volumes . . .

But I know what I like

Art museums do not have visiting hours for dogs. Much of what I know about art comes from hearsay or postcards. This applies to most people who discuss so glibly the pros and cons of modernism.

I admire unreservedly Henry Moore's abstract statuary near London's Serpentine. It suits Hyde Park as earrings do a gypsy. The patina is a joy. I have paid my respects to these works many times. I am sure he would approve.

I am a conservative in matters of art. We Cavaliers found our way to the canvases of great masters. This is because we seldom left the sides of Very Important Persons. And we are decorative. More so, in my opinion, than corgies or pugs, our rivals in the competition for honours as Top Dogs.

Many dogs are clumsy models. They do not know how to hold a pose in the studio. Great Danes, with their tongues hanging out, look as though they just failed to catch a hare.

I have never seen a dog in a Dutch painting who did not

behave like a slob about to gorge himself on fishheads and offal. With all that food around I don't actually blame them.

Stubbs's dogs are all right, but absent-minded. They always seem ready to jump out of the frame and start the chase.

Most French dogs in paintings are of mixed origins – no doubt the result of too many revolutions.

I don't recall seeing Chinese dogs but I am told that most of them end up on the spit rather than at art school.

A look at the catalogue

As a Cavalier I enjoy the thought that posterity will always remember me. My portrait has been painted many times. Just think of Watteau's *La Toilette* where three children and three adults ignore a stiff-jointed mandoline player and devote all their attention to a Cavalier puppy crawling towards a baby holding a sweet. A marvellous composition with all eyes focusing on the dog.

Same thing with *Cuyp's Landscape with a Horseman*. Eight people compete for our interest – nine counting the horse. Again here, all eyes focus on the Cavalier.

The sound of music

I grew up listening to music. It was felt, in what has been my home for many years, that the great classical works and operas fulfilled a useful function as tranquillizers. Whenever I was left alone in the flat a transistor set was switched on to keep me company. This accompaniment helped me through lonely hours but there can be too much of a good thing. As a result of this exposure to the Masters I find Mozart a bit soppy, Wagner pompous, but Elgar uplifting and evocative.

And the sound of poetry

Some of my best friends are writers. All of them have said

what needed to be said about dogs. But I am not sure I understand the meaning of Dylan Thomas when he writes: "Fog has a bone he'll trumpet into meat."

There is more, for me, in the lines of e. e. Cummings: "I am a birdcage without any bird, a collar looking for a dog, a kiss without lips." Sounds more friendly.

But I resent the cynicism of T. S. Eliot and his quatrain:

> "Now Dogs pretend they like to fight;
> They often bark, more seldom bite
> But yet a Dog is, on the whole,
> What you would call a simple soul."

I am sure I have demonstrated the absurdity of his cliché.

I have paid my respects to Henry Moore's abstracts again and again.

The Englishman's Debt to Dogdom and Vice Versa

> "Dogs are dogs, you sometimes think that they are not but they are. And they always are here, there and everywhere . . ."

GERTRUDE STEIN

Are we, the dogs of Britain, spoiling the English to the extent that they find us indispensable to their happiness?

The question has not yet been answered to everyone's satisfaction. It is not academic. We pay more attention to our people than we do to other canines. We even trust strangers on two legs more than we do our own kind on four. Something is wrong in the relationship. Not neatly balanced.

The Englishman owes a great deal to his dog. But his love for us can border on addiction. Far be it for me to suggest that we should help humans break the dog habit. But a little more aloofness might do us all some good.

The British are dependent on us. Just watch the man of the house in his armchair, reading his newspaper. Instinctively his free hand – the one not clutching the pipe or fumbling for the glass of malt whisky – descends towards the floor, groping for a furry brow. The fingers are ready to scratch.

If that hand does not find what it is looking for, the subsequent reaction is panic. Man must be weaned from dog.

We, the dogs, devote so much time to man that good works such as the R.S.P.C.A. or the Battersea Dogs' Home are neglected. It is as if our main function in life was to make humans happy. We should be thinking about social issues such as retraining, or relocation of abandoned animals. This will come. Meanwhile we must go on making sacrifices for our human companions.

So much to do, and so little time to do it!

We Cavaliers are more dedicated than any other breed to the tasks involved in the care, feeding and entertainment of man. Particularly in the following areas:

Health: Get them up early and see to it that they do not succumb to the temptation of a lie-in. I repeat that people need at least two hours' walk a day. Longevity is proportionate to the number of dogs that need exercise.

Morale: Humans are depressive. The Englishman in the morning takes top prizes for moroseness and gloom. We dispel fogs and hangovers with a few of our clown acts. We are good actors. Cheer-leaders if you will. Nothing is sadder than a dogless London dawn. We revive the old school spirit in our British friends. In these institutions which fill them with nostalgia to the rest of their days they learn to rise in the cold and in the dark and to brave the elements before breakfast. It is our role to stimulate the dormant Spartan mood, to melt away middle-age fat. All dogs, I confess, are not exactly raring to go when they hear the rain outside. Old dogs fall into ruts, human habits. But, on the whole, our native enthusiasm is catching.

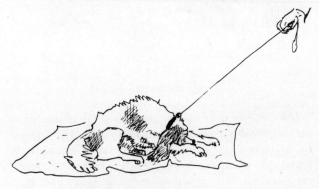

All dogs are not exactly raring to go

Communication: It is amazing how much time we must spend bringing people together. When we take them out they become aware of the need to return a smile and to engage in a discussion. Silence is a bad thing. Too much of it, I mean. Our barks enliven dead streets and give them the atmosphere of Catfish Row of Porgy and Bess fame.

Activity: We keep you people busy. Without us one might be inclined to waste hours on hobbies, model aeroplanes, stamp collecting. We help you face retirement. We are cheaper than psychoanalysts.

Finances: Thanks to us, man saves money. No Briton in his right mind would dream of wasting income on new furniture, carpets, curtains, where there are dogs around. We keep residences "lived in" the way most human males like them to be. Many country cottages look like outsize dog baskets full of frumpy cushions, scattered toys, rabbit tails.

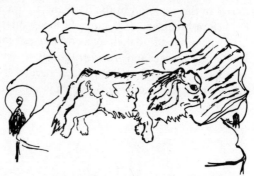

We keep residences "lived in"

Humour: We develop our people's sense of fun. Most games played by man today are ball games. They started the day man threw an apple down the lane and told dog to fetch it. There is no other explanation for cricket, tennis, even football. Why would so many run so fast and so far after a round object if we had not shown them how to?

[76]

Companionship: By nature, Englishmen and women are loners. The alternative to suicide was colonies, now exploration or yacht racing. The lonely Briton is dangerous to himself and, sometimes, to others. Unless dissuaded he rides camels in deserts and clambers up mountains. Present at his or her side, night and day, continuously, we prevent brooding. We have discouraged absurd adventures in virgin forests. Think of all the years wasted by Dr. Livingstone!

Perspective: We give man a sense of proportion he might lose if left to his own devices. We see to it that our problems overshadow his. We deter him from excessive involvement in politics. Behind every great man, every statesman, lies a faithful dog.

Keeping man occupied is no sinecure. It is true, perhaps, that too many responsibilities have been heaped on us, the dogs of Britain. But Top Dogs born close to the seat of power, in the corridors of it, never shrank from the task. Still, one day, man may have to learn to walk on his own two feet, without his favourite prop.

Dog's debt to the British

I am proud to be an English dog. My Welsh ancestry is an accident. I don't care much for rough, unsubtle terriers from the arid mountain slopes of Scotland and Wales.

The English have placed us on a pedestal and given us that halo of semi-godliness that suits us so well.

The lion and the unicorn have tried hard to displace us. But extinction has taken care of the latter and, with the help of poachers, it should soon settle the fate of the former.

Some people seek their national symbols in aviaries. We English dogs have a bulldog as spokesman.

Prosperity, poverty, technology, travelmania will not erode the Englishman's loyalty to dog. If things were to get worse the motto would again be "Very well then, alone . . . with my dog!"

Dog worship has deep roots in ancient history and mythology. In Ethiopia dogs were kings. When King Dog fawned upon the people this meant he was pleased with their behaviour. A growl betrayed displeasure with the handling of the affairs of the state. A little more of this here nowadays would help.

History may repeat itself. The cult of the dog may be revived. In the meantime man serves us as best he can, sometimes clumsily. Examples of devotion of man to dog abound. For instance:

– Man thinks of our welfare first. If *He* misses a step and falls all the way down the stairs, *She* asks, "Is the dog all right?" An instinctive reaction.

– Man and wife willingly give up privacy to satisfy our need for togetherness. Rare are the times when we find the bedroom door locked. Not for dogs such banalities as "three is a crowd".

– To demonstrate his aversion towards discrimination in hotels and restaurants, the Englishman will frequent cheap and grubby places where dogs are accepted.

– Humans neglect their health on our behalf. They often use our remedies and medicines instead of those the doctor prescribes for them.

– They travel third class or in baggage cars so that we shall not pine, alone in the dark.

– They give up holidays in the sun abroad to stay with us on this quarantined island. This way all of us can enjoy togetherness in glacial puddles and on rain-soaked beaches.

I could go on. Why should I? Man and dog are in each other's debt. I wish, however, the Creator had granted us equal lifespans. Dog's day is seven times shorter than man – therefore seven times fuller.

I Am a Londoner

> "But today you can no longer tell . . . You have to acquaint yourself with a civilization of which you disapprove, to appear to understand a thousand incomprehensible things . . ."
>
> M. MAETERLINCK – *My Dog*

Most Top Dogs are city dogs.

There are exceptions that prove the rule, but not many. The country dog is a hunter but a primitive. Only the city dog learns the tricks of survival in dangerous places. The street is, indeed, dangerous. The country dog wouldn't last long there.

Londoners, human as well as dogs, are inured to fumes, roaring lorries, loud talk. We call it Progress. We live dangerously. This is good for the soul.

The country dog melts into the environment. He lies in the sun and lets the flies play around his ears. He is taken for granted like an old carpet.

Such is the concern of humans for the city dog that life is an unending round of walks and outings. Together, the human and the dog, bound by the lead, go several times around the globe in a lifetime. This is a moving thought.

London at night! Driving to Fleet Street after dark, along the Embankment with the necklaces of lights on the bridges, and monocled Big Ben. Sheer magic. And the rumblings of trains overhead, the theatre crowds, the hearty welcome in bustling newspaper offices.

Meanwhile the country dog must content himself with the sound of horses munching oats in unlit barns, and with the hooting of owls.

London rain is softer than country rain, less harsh on man and beast. And there are havens in arcades and expensive stores. Country dog would not be seen dead in a raincoat.

My beautician is most skilful with brush and drier

London means transportation in private cars, taxis, buses even, the tube as a last resort. Taxis are built for dogs – roomy, clean, luxurious. Most cabbies are friendly to dogs.

Country dogs get baths now and then. In London the Top Dog goes to a beauty parlour. It is amazing what a session at *Town and Country*, my Salon, does for our morale.

[80]

My beautician is most skilful with brush and drier. I let her do things I would not allow anyone else try.

A city dog's bark echoes against walls and seldom goes unnoticed. Country bark is carried away by the wind. City dog barks at friend and foe. Country dog barks at ghosts.

Bands play in city parks to entertain London dogs. The only times I envy country dogs is when I go to the opera at Glyndebourne where picnic baskets dot the lawns as far as the nose can smell. True, we stay in the car park with the chauffeurs but it is worth the visit. And Glyndebourne audiences look particularly distinguished with all that dog hair on dinner jackets.

I am not saying that a few weeks in summer back to Nature isn't a pleasant change. But I have noticed that in the Cottage the dog loses some of his hard-won gains. It is as if he were downgraded, treated as somebody from the farmyard.

So I say, make it snappy. The sooner the bags get packed for the return journey, the better.

Life's Greatest Moments

"Animals talk to each other, of course. There can be no question about that; but I suppose there are very few people who can understand them."

MARK TWAIN – *A Tramp Abroad*

Man, who lives seven times longer than dog, is seven times less appreciative of happiness, seven times harder to please, seven times more indifferent to life's greatest moments.

Let me list the blessings that have come my way:

Mornings, when I am Top Dog in the street, having reached it first, finding it full of the treasures of the night. Just like beachcombing after a storm.

My Club: The group of friendly dogs waiting for me at the park gate, tails wagging.

Enemies: I have two, both dedicated. Six years ago I fought Sam, the wire-haired terrier, in single combat. Six stitches on my rump but the scar is on the soul. Every morning I shower insults on Sam from my balcony as he walks by. He hasn't had a good retort yet. After my cursing session I sink into my bean bag, exhausted, free of complexes for the day. The gentle art of making enemies.

Children: They come in many sizes and shapes. I am fond of the dog-size children aged about four or five. They are not yet spoilt. Their socks fall on their shoes. They smell of sticky foods. If one searches their pockets one finds half-sucked sweets. The trouble with them is that they have so many fingers, some of which are used to poke at dogs' eyes.

Very small children have no sense of balance. They collapse in a heap on the floor if pushed even slightly. Before they manage to get up their face can be licked and there are always remnants of ice-cream.

[82]

Children speak more clearly than adults who tend to use baby talk. They make great pets when they reach the ages of six to eleven. But, in Britain, they disappear for weeks at a time in kennels where their parents send them on obedience courses.

Floors: Top Dogs see a great deal of them. If, like myself, you are fully clothed in hair, the sensation of a marble floor under you on a hot day is wonderful. Marble is not available in the average home.

Fireplaces: Dogs are not supposed to be lying in front of fires for more than a few minutes. So say books on dog health. Pay no attention. I can't think of greater moments in life than those spent before the turf fire in my Irish cottage. Once in a while a handful of dry twigs is thrown on the grate and my dreams of hot pursuit after hares glow more brightly.

Beaches: Nothing like them anywhere in the world. If there is a Heaven it must be a beach, not a garden, a place where I can shake myself dry over the sandwiches and the glasses of Muscadet, raise my leg in a salute to a dead crab, wallow chin-deep in tidal puddles and venture into

I like children dog-size. But some of them have too many fingers

that other world, the upside-down world of salt water and foam.

Country lanes: The walk at sundown between hedgerows of blackberries, with the lovely smell of hay and herbs. But not at night when strangers prowl and sheepdogs dig out bones.

Beds: The beds human beings lie on, not easily accessible at first, but if we persevere we find our place between the two bodies and sleep as soundly as they do –

Admiration: Top Dogs needs it. Not vanity so much as the feeling that you are rewarded, like the actor after a fine performance. Some people are more liberal with flattery than others but, on the whole, the English do know how to find the right words to describe their dog's qualities. They wax lyrical about our blue ribbons.

Communications: The great moment when, after a year or two of training, humans master Dogspeak. All words are diminutives, much of the talk is nasal. We and they are on the same wavelength.

Teaching my people to speak my language

Girls: I have been introduced to nice Cavalier bitches. I don't know why their sex is called "opposite". The company of ladies seems to me necessary now and then although, like most Englishmen, I prefer male conversation.

The Street Where She Lived

> "I told her I loved her. I told her I should die without her. I told her that I idolized and worshipped her. Jip barked madly all the time."
>
> CHARLES DICKENS – *David Copperfield*

Someone – don't ask me who – has spread ugly rumours about the English being unwilling or afraid to discuss sex. This is quite untrue. They may be found any day of the year queuing up for tickets outside a theatre bearing a huge sign that screams NO SEX PLEASE, WE ARE BRITISH!

The truth is that they have two sets of standards: one for themselves, one for their dogs. They enjoy complete freedom of choice when it comes to their companion for a night of fun and frolic. Class barriers fall in the most mysterious way in the bedroom. Not for them all the talk about preserving the purity of the breed. But where dogs are concerned they, the masters, will not tolerate the slightest deviation from rules of conduct set by Puritan breeders.

On a shelf of the library in the house where I grew up are several books about the care and feeding of Cavaliers, each containing a chapter on "breeding". I wasn't meant to see these books but, being inquisitive by nature, I had a good look at them and I was shocked. They read like that other treatise on purity, MEIN KAMPF. Let me quote:

> "*How to set about being a breeder*
> Line breeding means breeding to a line and type rather than outcrossing all the time to outside lines. It is a good way to establish type but naturally must only be carried out with good, strong, healthy stock to be successful, and you must know your pedigrees well to carry it out."

[85]

Pray, tell me, is there any difference between this
strategy and Hitler's plans for a master race? But let me
quote further:

> "If you are going for breeding and showing do learn all
> you can, and I assure you there is a tremendous lot to
> learn about dogs and dog-breeding. It is only those who
> have been doing it for from three to five years who know
> it all. After that you begin to realise all the time how
> much more you have to learn . . . It is an extremely
> interesting hobby to take up and offers endless scope."

You must admit that the people who couch their
statements about intimate matters in such crude terms
should be locked up on charges of voyeurism. And here is
another example:

> "After the bitch has had a night to settle in she should
> then be introduced to the dog . . . she will be rather
> coquettish with him, probably going round him in
> circles and behaving very much like one is taught to
> believe Eve behaved to Adam."

There then follow two pages of unadulterated porno-
graphy which I wish to keep out of this book in case it falls
into the hands of children. Dog breeders must have coined
the expression "sex object", for this is exactly how they
regard us. And how fatuous this comment from an expert
on Cavaliers, respected by all in her profession but obviously blind to our needs:

> "Provided the mating has been satisfactory there is no
> need at all for a repetition."

By what authority is such a preposterous mis-statement
spread abroad? And who told the lady in my house that

She will be rather coquettish with him

mating would develop insatiable appetites in me, her prize possession, her closest friend? It had been decided from the time of adoption that I would never be exposed to the things of the flesh . . . whatever that may mean.

Wisely or not, I decided that some day, somewhere, if opportunity knocked, I would do my own thing. To cut a long story short, it happened in broad daylight in the very heart of London. But let us not anticipate.

Had the events I am about to relate come to the attention of the unsavoury type known as the *investigative reporter*, the headline in afternoon newspapers would have read *TOP DOG HITS BOTTOM!* Or, perhaps, *COVENT GARDEN MATING SHOCK*.

[87]

But, of course, the denizens of Fleet Street were busy bending the elbow in sleazy pubs. And so I must tell my own story.

It started on a hot day in May when I befriended a mongrel bitch in the eastern reaches of Hyde Park. It was love at first sight. Eve had nothing to teach her. I slipped out of my Vuitton collar and gave chase. Despite her unkempt appearance and a coat that could have done with a good brushing, the temptress was graceful, fast on her feet and quick-witted.

In all of us there is a devil asleep. She aroused the devil in me. I forgot all I had learned in the human world, the world I had left to precipitously that loyalty to man evaporated.

How she knew her way around London! I followed her through unfamiliar streets. She was luring me away from everything I held sacred . . . and I didn't care.

That is how I found myself in a narrow passageway near Rose Street, Covent Garden, with a strange playmate. What passed between us is not for publication (I think politicians and spokesmen call it *off the record*). Suffice it to say that I was swept off my feet. Anyway, my front feet. The world around us whirled . . .

When I came to my senses she was gone, I was leadless, collarless, in a part of the city devoid of familiar olfactory landmarks. Any other dog would have lost his composure. True to my Cavalier traditions I remained calm and I surveyed the situation.

There was writing on the wall in that dark lane bearing the name of *Lamb and Flag*. It said that "*Hard by was enacted the notorious Rose Alley Ambuscade in December 1679, the Poet Dryden was almost done to death at the instance of Louise de Keroualle, Mistress of Charles II*".

Incredible coincidence! I had landed in a part of London impregnated with history, *my* history. This was King Charles Cavalier territory *par excellence*.

Moved to tears at the thought of surfacing from the bottomless pit of carnal sin on the very spot where the masters and mistresses of my ancestors had avenged their honour, I trotted round the corner into more history: King Street, Henrietta Street, streets with a past. On an elegant building I saw the motto of a famous ducal family *Que Sera Sera*. Yes, what will be will be. Yet, in the case of Covent Garden, the appropriate slogan is *What has been has been*.

Few districts are so haunted by ghosts

For readers who don't know the place, few districts are so haunted by ghosts. The ghosts of the market ladies of yore who "stunk so of brandy, strong drink and tobacco", the ghosts of more recent, and no doubt fairer, flower ladies who fell in love with professors, married them and, I am sure, lived unhappily ever after with these confirmed bachelors.

Covent Garden, once a world where barrows rumbled on cobblestones, where the ground was coated with a mixture of mud, crushed banana, crankcase oil, tea leaves and pigeon droppings. A food market now gone. A place about which Thackeray wrote that it had "a population that never seems to sleep and does all in its power to prevent others from sleeping".

Covent Garden, having lost an empire, has not yet

[89]

found a role. So it has made more room for decorators and ghosts. The ghost of Dickens who came here as a child to stare at pineapples. Of Voltaire in exile after serving time in the Bastille, the ghosts of Shaw, Hogarth, Coleridge, Pope, Locke, Newton, Addison.

But I have strayed from my subject.

The subject, if memory serves, was sex and the British. Or sex and the Cavalier. How it led so quickly to culture, history and archaeology, I am not sure. But this should please my American readers.

Although I was lost, hungry and somewhat apprehensive about the consequences of my brief encounter with a loose bitch, I had time to reflect about the lions of British letters who had so little to do that they could afford to spend so much time away from their writing table or easels to mix with Covent Garden marketeers, minding other people's businesses, getting hit over the head by the hired hands of royal harlots.

This is a story with a happy ending.

As I sniffed my way around Covent Garden I met people, not only ghosts. People stop when they see a dog without a collar and lead, alone, apparently helpless. They don't stop for other people in the same condition.

I met a woman pushing a baby carriage filled with primroses who was muttering something about the rains in Spain. I met a gipsy in tweeds and red waistcoat who parked cars for opera-addicts. I met other kinds of addicts who didn't know where they were. I met winos who slept rough under the bushes outside St. Paul's Covent Garden. I slept rough with them. In the morning one of them spoke the words that eventually got me my freedom. He got up, stretched, and said that "there must be a reward".

There was a reward. By then all police stations had been alerted. My description was on the telex machines. Specialists were working on my identikit picture.

Specialists were working on my identikit picture

Early that morning, at Bow Street police headquarters, I was reunited with the hands that feed me, with the only people who matter: Dog's best friends.

Conclusion . . . in the Form of "Q" and "A"

Interviewer

All right, McMuck, you have had your say. You won't mind if we who share your life put a few questions to you?

McMuck

Not at all, dear boy, fire away

Interviewer

In your last venture to the brink of disaster you seem to have forgotten all about loyalty to man. You become a stray. All of this on impulse. How do you expect us to believe such a tale?

McMuck

No book is complete without "film content". Can you think of a movie with a credible love story? Even a dog knows that you don't write books for readers but for the film rights.

Interviewer

So, there is a venal streak in you?

McMuck

Don't be silly. Would I be modern if there wasn't?

Interviewer

You will be criticized for being class-conscious. Why do you divide dogdom into higher and lower classes and according to purity of strain?

McMuck

I must have learned this from humans. I am English, you know. I believe in THEM and US. There is no room for dogs in egalitarian societies.

Interviewer

Would you call yourself a male chauvinist?

McMuck

Certainly. There is no room for dogs in societies which

send women to the factory or the office. A woman's place is . . .

Interviewer

I know, I know. Still, the title TOP DOG strikes even your most ardent admirers as arrogant.

McMuck

Can you give me a single example of the meek having inherited anything, let alone the earth? Arrogance is the key to success for man and beast . . . except for salesmen. I have nothing to sell.

Interviewer

So you would describe yourself as a snob, and proud of it?

McMuck

Top Dogs are arrogant, not snobbish. The snob is an individual unsure of the thickness and quality of his veneer. One is born arrogant. One becomes a snob on one's way up.

Interviewer

Is there not a good deal of nonsense in what you write about the English?

McMuck

You may be right. Writing about ourselves is a national habit, isn't it?

Interviewer

What makes you so sure that the dog is not on his way out?

McMuck

Ridiculous! Just read the statistics. The pet food industry grows year after year.

Interviewer

And you don't feel guilty at the thought of all that food going to the dogs in a world where millions starve?

McMuck

I learned at my mother's knee what she learned at her mother's knee: that human starvation is man-made, the result or the cause of war, negligence, injustice. Why hold dogs responsible?

Interviewer

In the preceding chapters you imply that the English dog can teach his English master any trick. Are you sure?

McMuck

I don't like the word "Master". I am satisfied that the special relationship between man and dog on these islands is exceptionally close. It amounts to virtual transmutation or, of you prefer, to reincarnation before death.

Interviewer

And yet the statisticians you were quoting a moment ago tell us that France boasts a dog population of 8.2 million, as against Britain's 5.2 million. And the French spend as much on their dogs every year as they do on their diplomats.

McMuck

Is this not as it should be?

Interviewer

Perhaps. But what makes you so sure the dog is not a passing fad?

McMuck

That is what they said about the motor-car and the aeroplane. In fact we become more indispensable to humans as tensions grow in the world. American psychiatrists have found that animal presence "tranquillizes" persons with a psychosomatic cardiovascular condition. Pat a dog and watch your blood pressure go down.

Interviewer

One more question. Do you always have the last word?

McMuck

There is no last word in the century of mass communications.

Glossary

The following are words often used by humans but obviously taken from dog language. This list of kennel sounds is compiled as our contribution to research in languages.

C. M. McMuck

Alf	Off	Roughage	Warfare
Bough	Oof	Ruff	Whop
Bow	RAAF	Ruffle	Whoop
Haft	Raft	WAAF	Wolf
Half	Ralph	Waffle	Woof
Harp	Ref	Waif	Wow
Hoop	Roof	Warp	
Gruff	Rough	Wharf	

From the French: Boeuf, Oeuf, Veuf. From the German: Auf, Hof, Huf